D1066224

Contents

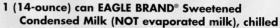
Fruit Smoothies

**1 (14-ounce) can EAGLE BRAND® Sweetened
  Condensed Milk (NOT evaporated milk), chilled**
1 (8-ounce) carton plain yogurt
1 small banana, cut up
1 cup frozen or fresh whole strawberries
**1 (8-ounce) can crushed pineapple packed in juice,
  chilled**
2 tablespoons lemon juice
1 cup ice cubes

In blender container, combine chilled EAGLE BRAND®, yogurt,
banana, whole strawberries, pineapple with its juice and lemon
juice; cover and blend until smooth. With blender running,
gradually add ice cubes, blending until smooth. Serve
immediately. *Makes 5 servings*

Key Lime Smoothies: Omit strawberries, pineapple and
lemon juice. Add ⅓ cup key lime juice from concentrate.
Proceed as directed above. Tint with green food coloring,
if desired.

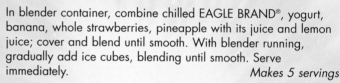

4 Berry Good

Sparkling Strawberry Float

2 tablespoons pink decorative sugar (optional)
2 cups (8 ounces) frozen unsweetened strawberries
1 container (6 ounces) strawberry yogurt
½ cup milk
2 tablespoons honey or sugar
2 scoops strawberry sorbet

1. Place sugar in small shallow dish. Wet rims of glasses with damp paper towel; dip into sugar. Place glasses upright to dry.

2. Place strawberries, yogurt, milk and honey in blender. Cover; blend until smooth. Divide between prepared glasses. Top each glass with scoop of strawberry sorbet. *Makes 2 servings*

Red Raspberry Smoothie

⅔ cup frozen red raspberries, partially thawed*
½ cup milk
½ cup vanilla frozen yogurt
¼ teaspoon vanilla
Whole red raspberries (optional)

*To partially thaw raspberries, place them in a small bowl and microwave on LOW for 1 minute.

1. Place raspberries and milk in blender. Cover; process 10 to 15 seconds. To remove seeds, strain mixture through sieve into small bowl; return strained mixture to blender.

2. Add frozen yogurt and vanilla to blender. Cover; process 10 to 15 seconds or until mixture is smooth. Pour into glass. Garnish with raspberries. Serve immediately.

Makes 1 serving

Strawberry-Banana Yogurt Energy Drink

**1 box (10 ounces) BIRDS EYE® frozen Strawberries,
   partially thawed
2 medium bananas
¾ cup plain yogurt**

• Place all ingredients in blender or food processor; blend until
smooth.   *Makes 2½ cups*

Serving Suggestion: Add 2 teaspoons wheat germ or ¼ cup
fruit juice.

Nectarine Mocktail

3 fresh California nectarines, halved, pitted and diced
1 container (10 ounces) unsweetened frozen
    strawberries, partially thawed
1 bottle (28 ounces) club soda or sugar-free ginger ale
8 mint sprigs (optional)

Add nectarines, strawberries and 1 cup club soda to blender. Process until smooth. Pour into chilled glasses about ⅔ full. Top with remaining club soda. Garnish with mint, if desired.

Makes 8 servings

Favorite recipe from **California Tree Fruit Agreement**

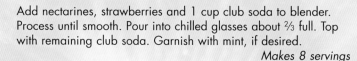

Strawberry Delights

2 cups strawberry ice cream
1 cup sliced fresh strawberries
⅔ cup cold milk
¼ cup cold orange juice
⅛ teaspoon ground cinnamon

1. Place all ingredients in blender or food processor. Cover; blend at high speed until smooth.

2. Pour into glasses. Garnish as desired. Serve immediately.

Makes 4 servings

Banana-Pineapple Breakfast Shake

2 cups plain yogurt
1 can (8 ounces) crushed pineapple in juice, undrained
1 medium ripe banana
8 packets sugar substitute
1 teaspoon vanilla
⅛ teaspoon ground nutmeg
1 cup ice cubes

1. Place all ingredients in blender. Cover; blend at medium speed until smooth.

2. Pour into glasses; serve immediately.   *Makes 4 servings*

Frozen Florida Monkey Malt

2 bananas
1 cup milk
5 tablespoons frozen orange juice concentrate
3 tablespoons malted milk powder

1. Wrap peeled bananas in plastic wrap; freeze.

2. Break bananas into pieces; place in blender with milk, orange juice concentrate and malted milk powder. Blend until smooth.

3. Pour into glasses; serve immediately.   *Makes 2 servings*

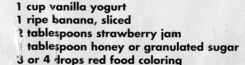

Valentine Smoothie

1 cup vanilla yogurt
1 ripe banana, sliced
2 tablespoons strawberry jam
1 tablespoon honey or granulated sugar
3 or 4 drops red food coloring

Combine all ingredients in blender. Cover; blend at high speed 20 seconds or until foamy.

Pour into glasses. Garnish as desired. Serve immediately.

Makes 2 servings

Tip: Change the flavors of this recipe to make it a year-round treat. Substitute your favorite flavor of yogurt and use any fruit combination, such as a mix of frozen berries or cherries.

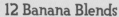

Strawberry-Banana Smoothie

**2 cups fresh or frozen unsweetened strawberries,
  hulled**
2 bananas, sliced
1 container (8 ounces) low-fat vanilla yogurt
½ cup skim milk
¼ cup rice bran
3 tablespoons lemon juice
1 to 2 tablespoons honey

Cover and freeze strawberries and sliced bananas until firm, about 4 hours or overnight. Combine strawberries, bananas, yogurt, milk, bran, lemon juice and honey in blender; process until smooth. Serve immediately in chilled serving glasses.

Makes 4 servings

Favorite recipe from **USA Rice**

Fruit 'n Juice Breakfast Shake

1 extra-ripe, medium DOLE® Banana
¾ cup DOLE® Pineapple Juice
½ cup lowfat vanilla yogurt
½ cup DOLE® Fresh Frozen Blueberries

Combine all ingredients in blender. Process until smooth.

Makes 2 servings

Banana Smoothies & Pops

**1 (14-ounce) can EAGLE BRAND® Sweetened
  Condensed Milk (NOT evaporated milk)
1 (8-ounce) container vanilla yogurt
2 ripe bananas
½ cup orange juice**

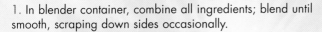

1. In blender container, combine all ingredients; blend until
smooth, scraping down sides occasionally.

2. Serve immediately. Store leftovers covered in refrigerator.

Makes 4 cups

Banana Smoothie Pops: Spoon banana mixture into
8 (5-ounce) paper cups. Freeze 30 minutes. Insert wooden craft
sticks into center of each cup; freeze until firm.

Fruit Smoothies: Substitute 1 cup of your favorite fruit and
½ cup any fruit juice for banana and orange juice.

Kiwi Strawberry Smoothie

2 kiwi, peeled and sliced
1 cup frozen whole unsweetened strawberries
1 container (6 ounces) strawberry yogurt
½ cup milk
2 tablespoons honey

1. Place all ingredients in blender. Cover; process 15 to 30 seconds until smooth, using on/off pulsing action to break up chunks.

2. Pour into glasses; serve immediately.   *Makes 2 servings*

Soy Kiwi Strawberry Smoothie: Substitute 1 container (6 ounces) strawberry soy yogurt for regular strawberry yogurt.

Caribbean Dream

¾ cup vanilla ice cream
¾ cup pineapple sherbet
¾ cup tropical fruit salad, drained
¼ cup frozen banana-orange juice concentrate
¼ teaspoon rum extract

1. Place all ingredients in blender. Blend 1 to 2 minutes or until smooth and well blended.

2. Pour into glasses; serve immediately.   *Makes 2 servings*

Lighten Up: To reduce the fat, replace vanilla ice cream with reduced-fat or fat-free ice cream or frozen yogurt.

Cranberry Pineapple Smoothie

2 cups Cranberry Pineapple Smoothie Base
   (recipe follows)
1 large ripe banana (optional)
4 cups ice cubes
   Orange peel and mint leaves (optional)

1. Prepare Cranberry Pineapple Smoothie Base.

2. In blender combine 2 cups Smoothie Base and banana; process until smooth.

3. With blender running, add ice cubes, several at a time. Process until thick and smooth. If desired, garnish with orange peel and mint leaves. *Makes about 6 servings*

Cranberry Pineapple Smoothie Base

1 cup KARO® Light Corn Syrup
1 can (16 ounces) whole berry cranberry sauce
1 can (8 ounces) crushed pineapple in unsweetened
   juice, undrained

In blender combine all ingredients; process until smooth. Store covered in refrigerator up to 1 week. *Makes 4 cups base*

Piña Colada Punch

3 cups water
10 whole cloves
4 cardamom pods
2 cinnamon sticks
1 can (12 ounces) frozen pineapple juice concentrate, thawed
1 pint piña colada frozen yogurt or pineapple sherbet, softened
1¼ cups lemon seltzer water
1¼ teaspoons rum extract
¾ teaspoon coconut extract

Combine water, cloves, cardamom and cinnamon in saucepan. Bring to a boil over high heat; reduce heat to low. Simmer, covered, 5 minutes; cool. Strain; discard spices. Combine spiced water, pineapple juice concentrate and yogurt in pitcher. Stir until yogurt is melted. Stir in seltzer water, rum extract and coconut extract.   Makes 10 to 12 servings

Kiwi Pineapple Cream

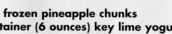

1 cup frozen pineapple chunks
1 container (6 ounces) key lime yogurt
1 kiwi, peeled and sliced
½ cup canned unsweetened coconut milk
1 tablespoon honey

1. Place all ingredients in blender. Cover; process 15 to 30 seconds until smooth, using on/off pulsing action to break up chunks.

2. Pour into glasses; serve immediately.   *Makes 2 servings*

Kiwi Chai Smoothie: Add ¼ teaspoon vanilla, ⅛ teaspoon cardamom, ⅛ teaspoon ground cinnamon, ⅛ teaspoon ground ginger and a pinch of cloves to the mixture before blending.

Tropical Breeze Smoothie

1 cup frozen pineapple chunks
1 cup frozen mango chunks
½ cup canned unsweetened coconut milk
½ cup milk
2 tablespoons honey

1. Place all ingredients in blender. Cover; process 15 to 30 seconds or until smooth, using on/off pulsing action to break up chunks.

2. Pour into glasses; serve immediately.   *Makes 2 servings*

Apricot Peachy Chiller

1 can (about 9 ounces) apricots in heavy syrup
1 cup cut-up frozen peach slices
½ cup frozen whole unsweetened strawberries
1 container (6 ounces) vanilla yogurt
1 to 2 tablespoons fresh lemon juice (optional)

1. Place all ingredients in blender. Cover; process 15 to 30 seconds until smooth, using on/off pulsing action to break up chunks.

2. Pour into glasses; serve immediately.   *Makes 3 servings*

Soy Apricot Peachy Chiller: Substitute 1 container (6 ounces) vanilla or peach soy yogurt for regular vanilla yogurt.

Cherry Chocolate Frosty

1 container (6 ounces) chocolate yogurt
½ cup frozen dark sweet cherries
⅛ to ¼ teaspoon almond extract

1. Place all ingredients in blender. Cover; process 15 to 30 seconds until smooth, using on/off pulsing action to break up chunks.

2. Pour into glass; serve immediately.   *Makes 1 serving*

Peachy Chocolate Yogurt Shake

⅔ cup peeled fresh peach slices *or* 1 package (10 ounces) frozen peach slices, thawed and drained
¼ teaspoon almond extract
2 cups (1 pint) vanilla nonfat frozen yogurt
¼ cup HERSHEY'S Syrup
¼ cup nonfat milk

Place peaches and almond extract in blender container. Cover; blend until smooth. Add frozen yogurt, syrup and milk. Cover; blend until smooth. Serve immediately.   *Makes 4 servings*

Creamy Fruit Blend

1 cup milk
½ cup white grape juice
½ cup fresh or frozen unsweetened strawberries
1 small ripe peach, peeled, pitted and quartered
1 ripe banana, peeled and quartered
2 tablespoons brown sugar
1 tablespoon lemon juice
½ teaspoon almond extract
Fresh fruit for garnish (optional)

1. Place all ingredients in blender. Cover; blend until smooth.

2. Pour into glasses; garnish as desired. Serve immediately.

Makes 2 to 3 servings

Peachy Keen Smoothie

2 cups frozen sliced peaches
1 container (6 ounces) peach yogurt
½ cup milk
¼ teaspoon vanilla

1. Place all ingredients in blender container. Cover; blend until smooth.

2. Pour into glasses; serve immediately.   *Makes 2 servings*

Orange Smoothies

1 cup vanilla ice cream or vanilla frozen yogurt
¾ cup milk
¼ cup frozen orange juice concentrate

1. Combine all ingredients in blender. Cover; blend until smooth.

2. Pour into glasses; serve immediately.   *Makes 2 servings*

Tofu Orange Dream

½ cup soft tofu
½ cup orange juice
1 container (about 2½ ounces) baby food carrots
2 tablespoons honey *or* 1 tablespoon sugar
¼ teaspoon fresh grated ginger
2 to 3 ice cubes

1. Place all ingredients in blender. Cover; blend 15 seconds until smooth.

2. Pour into glass; serve immediately.   *Makes 1 serving*

Soy Mango Smoothie

1 cup frozen mango chunks
1 container (6 ounces) vanilla soy yogurt
½ cup orange juice
2 tablespoons honey
⅛ to ¼ teaspoon grated fresh ginger

1. Place all ingredients in blender. Cover; process 30 to
45 seconds or until mixture is smooth, using on/off pulsing
action to break up chunks.

2. Pour into glasses; serve immediately.   *Makes 2 servings*

Berry Soy-Cream Blend

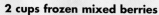

2 cups frozen mixed berries
1 can (14 ounces) blackberries, with juice
1 cup (8 ounces) almond milk or soy milk
1 cup apple juice
½ cup (4 ounces) soft tofu enriched with calcium

1. Place all ingredients in blender. Cover; blend on high speed until smooth.

2. Pour into glasses; serve immediately.   *Makes 2 servings*

Tofu Peanut Butter Smoothie

1 banana, cut into chunks
½ cup soft tofu
¼ cup creamy peanut butter
2 tablespoons honey *or* 1 tablespoon sugar
1 teaspoon vanilla
1 to 2 ice cubes

1. Place all ingredients in blender. Cover; process 15 to 30 seconds until smooth, using on/off pulsing action to break up ice.

2. Pour into glass; serve immediately.   *Makes 1 serving*

Soy Milk Smoothie

3 cups plain or vanilla soy milk
1 banana, peeled and frozen (see Tip)
1 cup frozen strawberries or raspberries
1 teaspoon vanilla or almond extract
⅓ cup EQUAL® SPOONFUL*

*May substitute 8 packets EQUAL® sweetener.

• Place all ingredients in blender or food processor. Blend until smooth.   *Makes 4 servings*

Tip: Peel and cut banana into large chunks. Place in plastic freezer bag, seal and freeze at least 5 to 6 hours or overnight.

Tofu Fruit & Veggie Smoothie

1 cup frozen pineapple chunks
½ cup soft tofu
½ cup apple juice
½ cup orange juice
1 container (about 2½ ounces) baby food carrots

1. Place all ingredients in blender. Cover; process 15 to 30 seconds until smooth, using on/off pulsing action to break up chunks.

2. Pour into glasses; serve immediately.   *Makes 2 servings*

Slimming Chocoberry Splash

Crushed ice
¾ cup cold nonfat milk
¼ cup sliced fresh strawberries
2 tablespoons HERSHEY'S Syrup
2 tablespoons vanilla ice milk
2 tablespoons club soda

1. Fill two tall glasses with crushed ice.

2. Place all remaining ingredients except club soda in blender container. Cover; blend until smooth. Pour into glasses over crushed ice; add club soda. Serve immediately. Garnish as desired. *Makes 2 servings*

Variation: Substitute any of the following for strawberries: ⅓ cup drained canned peach slices, 3 tablespoons frozen raspberries, 2 pineapple slices or ¼ cup drained crushed canned pineapple.

Mango Batido

1 large mango
1¾ cups milk
2 tablespoons frozen orange-peach-mango
   juice concentrate
4 ice cubes
⅛ teaspoon almond extract

1. Peel mango. Cut fruit away from pit; cut fruit into cubes.

2. Combine all ingredients in blender; blend until smooth. Pour
into glasses; serve immediately.   *Makes 4 servings*

Tip: Chill mango before preparing recipe or use frozen mango
pieces.

Rockin' Raspberry Refresher

¼ cup fresh or thawed frozen unsweetened raspberries
2 tablespoons frozen pink lemonade concentrate
1 cup club soda, chilled, divided

1. Place raspberries and lemonade concentrate in blender. Cover; blend on high speed until smooth. Add ¼ cup club soda to blender. Cover; blend until mixed.

2. Pour remaining ¾ cup club soda in a tall glass. Pour in raspberry mixture; stir and serve. *Makes 1 serving*

Orange Banana Nog

1 cup orange juice
½ cup fat-free milk
½ cup no-cholesterol real egg product
1 small banana, sliced
2 to 3 tablespoons EQUAL® SPOONFUL*
Ground nutmeg

*May substitute 3 to 4½ packets EQUAL® sweetener.

• Blend all ingredients except nutmeg in blender or food processor until smooth; pour into glasses. Sprinkle lightly with nutmeg.   *Makes 4 servings*

The Luscious Pink One

4 fresh California peaches, peeled, halved,
**   pitted and sliced**
1 cup buttermilk
½ cup strawberries (or other red berries)
1 tablespoon lemon juice
Strawberries for garnish

Add peaches, buttermilk, strawberries and lemon juice to food processor or blender. Process until smooth. Pour into 4 mugs. Freeze until slushy. Top each serving with strawberry, if desired. Serve immediately with long-handled spoons and straws.

Makes 4 servings

Favorite recipe from **California Tree Fruit Agreement**

Mocha Cooler

1 cup milk
¼ cup vanilla or coffee ice cream
1 tablespoon instant coffee granules
1 tablespoon chocolate syrup

1. Place all ingredients in blender container. Cover; process until smooth.

2. Pour into serving glass; garnish as desired. Serve immediately.

Makes 1 serving

Banana Split Shakes

1 small (6-inch) ripe banana
¼ cup skim milk
5 maraschino cherries, drained
1 tablespoon chocolate syrup
⅛ teaspoon coconut extract
4 cups chocolate frozen yogurt

1. Combine banana, milk, cherries, chocolate syrup and coconut extract in blender. Cover; blend on high until smooth.

2. Add yogurt 1 cup at a time. Cover; pulse blend on high after each addition until smooth and thick. Pour into glasses; serve immediately.   *Makes 4 servings*

Tip: For a low-fat shake, chop 3 large, peeled bananas. Freeze until solid. Blend with milk, cherries, chocolate syrup and coconut extract.

Chocolate Mint Cooler

2 cups cold whole milk or half-and-half
¼ cup chocolate syrup
1 teaspoon peppermint extract
Crushed ice
Aerosol whipped cream
Mint leaves

1. Combine milk, chocolate syrup and peppermint extract in small pitcher; stir until well blended.

2. Fill 2 serving glasses with crushed ice. Pour milk mixture over ice. Top with whipped cream. Garnish with mint leaves.

Makes about 2 servings

Iced Creamy Chai

2 spiced chai-flavored tea bags
1 cup boiling water
   Ice cubes
½ cup cream, divided
2 cups cool water, divided
2 packets no calorie sweetener (or 2 tablespoons
   sucralose-based sugar substitute), divided
   Ground cinnamon or nutmeg (optional)

1. Steep both tea bags in boiling water for about 4 minutes to brew 1 cup double-strength tea. Remove tea bags; refrigerate to cool.

2. Pour half of cooled tea (less than ½ cup) over ice in each of 2 tall glasses. Add ¼ cup cream, 1 cup cool water and 1 packet sweetener to each glass; stir to combine. Sprinkle with cinnamon just before serving.   *Makes 2 servings*

Shamrock Smoothies

1 ripe banana, peeled and cut into chunks
1 cup ice cubes
¾ cup apple juice
¼ cup plain yogurt
½ teaspoon vanilla
¼ teaspoon orange extract
2 or 3 drops green food coloring

1. Place all ingredients in blender or food processor; blend until smooth and frothy.

2. Pour into glasses; serve immediately. *Makes 2 servings*

Peanut Butter & Jelly Shakes

1½ cups vanilla ice cream
¼ cup milk
2 tablespoons creamy peanut butter
6 peanut butter sandwich cookies, coarsely chopped
¼ cup strawberry preserves

1. Place ice cream, milk and peanut butter in blender. Blend at medium speed 1 to 2 minutes or until smooth and well blended. Add chopped cookies; blend 10 seconds at low speed. Pour into 2 serving glasses.

2. Place preserves and 1 to 2 teaspoons water in small bowl; stir until smooth. Stir 2 tablespoons preserve mixture into each glass. Serve immediately. *Makes 2 servings*

Iced Cappuccino

1 cup vanilla frozen yogurt or vanilla ice cream
1 cup cold strong-brewed coffee
2 teaspoons sugar
1 teaspoon unsweetened cocoa powder
1 teaspoon vanilla

1. Place all ingredients in food processor or blender; process until smooth. Place container in freezer; freeze 1½ to 2 hours or until top and sides of mixture are partially frozen.

2. Scrape sides of container; process until smooth and frothy. Pour into glasses; serve immediately. *Makes 2 servings*

Iced Mocha Cappuccino: Increase amount of unsweetened cocoa powder to 1 tablespoon. Proceed as above.

Tip: To add an extra flavor boost, add orange peel, lemon peel or a dash of ground cinnamon to the coffee grounds before brewing.

Purple Cow

3 cups vanilla frozen yogurt
1 cup milk
½ cup thawed frozen grape juice concentrate
    (undiluted)
1½ teaspoons lemon juice

1. Place all ingredients in blender or food processor; blend until smooth.

2. Pour into glasses; serve immediately.   *Makes 6 servings*

Razzmatazz Shake: Place 1 quart vanilla frozen yogurt, 1 cup vanilla yogurt and ¼ cup chocolate syrup in food processor; process until smooth. Pour ½ of mixture evenly into 12 glasses; top with ½ can (12 ounces) root beer. Fill glasses equally with remaining yogurt mixture; top with remaining root beer. Makes 12 (⅔-cup) servings.

Sunshine Shake: Place 1 quart vanilla nonfat frozen yogurt, 1⅓ cups orange juice, 1 cup fresh or thawed frozen raspberries and 1 teaspoon sugar in food processor; process until smooth. Pour into 10 glasses; sprinkle with nutmeg. Makes 10 (½-cup) servings.

Acknowledgments

The publisher would like to thank the companies and organizations listed below for the use of their recipes and photographs in this publication.

ACH Food Companies, Inc.

Birds Eye Foods

California Tree Fruit Agreement

Dole Food Company, Inc.

EAGLE BRAND®

Equal® sweetener

The Hershey Company

USA Rice Federation